BEHIND GOLD DOORS

FIVE LEGENDS OFFER THE KEYS TO EMPOWERING LEADERSHIP

Lonnie Pacelli

Published by Pacelli Publishing
Bellevue, Washington

Pacelli
PUBLISHING

BEHIND GOLD DOORS
FIVE LEGENDS OFFER THE KEYS TO EMPOWERING LEADERSHIP

Published by Pacelli Publishing
9905 Lake Washington Blvd. NE, #D-103
Bellevue, Washington 98004
PacelliPublishing.com

ISBN-10: 1-933750-80-4
ISBN-13: 978-1-933750-80-4

Embossed Card

S am had been dreading this meeting for days. He stood outside Karen's office waiting for her to finish her phone conversation. He could see her through the window in her door. She held up her index finger. Only one more minute before the dressing-down.

Karen hung up the phone and motioned Sam in.

"How's it going?" Sam said.

"Fine, thanks."

Karen got up from her desk and sat at a small round table with two chairs. Sam sat across from her and put his notebook and water bottle on the table.

"Sam, have you had a chance to review your performance appraisal?"

Sam opened his notebook. In it was a folded copy of the appraisal.

"I have."

"Good. Let's talk through strengths and areas for improvement."

Sam had always been an over-achiever. Graduating from college at age 20, he took great pride in how much he achieved at such a young age. He had been considered a rising star at the company since joining five years earlier. He was recently promoted to a management position, with an organization of ten people reporting to him. This was his first performance appraisal as a manager.

"So, let's first go through strengths," Karen said. Sam barely looked at the strengths, it was that one area for improvement that dominated his thoughts.

Karen continued. "Great delivery results, you come in on budget, customer satisfaction exceeds expectations. Great work." Karen continued with more specifics and comments from customers. Sam sat quietly as she talked, giving an occasional nod and *mm-hmm* to signal understanding.

"Enough with this, get on with the meat," he thought.

"Great, now let's talk about areas for improvement."

Sam leaned back in his chair, his hands gripping the armrests.

"Your organization's employee satisfaction surveys raised something we need to work on together."

Sam looked back at his manager score on the appraisal where his score was compared to other managers in the company. His score was among the lowest, with 95 percent of the managers scoring higher than him. It was the first time in his career he wasn't at the top of the heap, let alone being in the lowest five percent.

"In looking at the questions and comments, people seem concerned about your ability to empower others."

This was a total shock to Sam. He thought he did a great job of delegating and getting things done with his team. It wasn't just one person who said he didn't delegate effectively; it was a consensus among his team.

"I just don't understand this," Sam stammered. "I work so hard to make sure I am delegating work effectively." Karen and Sam continued to talk through the employee survey. To Karen, this was something for Sam to work on in his leadership journey. To Sam, it was like having bamboo stuck under his fingernails. Karen saw how this was impacting Sam; so she decided to make him an offer.

"Sam, you have great potential, and I want to ensure I'm doing my part to help you grow as a leader." Karen got up from the table, went back to her desk, opened the top drawer, took out a gold card, and sat back down at the table.

"There is a very special empowerment class I would like you to attend," Karen said as she handed him the card.

Sam looked at the card, a gold embossed door on the front, an address on the back. He recognized the address.

"This is a bakery; you want me to go to a class at a bakery?"

"Take tomorrow off. Go to the address on the card. They'll be waiting for you."

"Um, okay," Sam said. He had thought for sure he would be fired. Instead he was being sent to a class. Sam got up from the table, grateful he still had his job but perplexed by the gold card and what awaited him the next day.

"Thank you, Karen."

"Hang in there Sam, and let's get together after the class to talk about what you've learned."

"Okay." Sam left her office. As he walked to his office, he ran his thumb over the outline of the door on the embossed card. He flipped it over and looked at the address again.

"A bakery?"

The Elevator

Eighteen Claire Place. Sam stopped there every day for a blueberry muffin and coffee. As he approached the address, he saw a small plain single-story white building where the bakery stood just yesterday. He looked at the address on the card and flipped it over to see the embossed door. It was identical to the door on the strange white building.

"What the..." He said to himself. He opened the door and went inside. A man in gray pants and a navy sport coat sat on a folding chair against the wall, head down reading a newspaper. A gold elevator was at the far end of the entry, flanked by white walls, ceiling, and a white marble floor.

"Welcome, Sam," the man said, his eyes still focused on his reading.

"Thank you." Sam walked toward the man to shake his hand, but the man just sat there, both hands on the newspaper, never raising his gaze.

"Go to the elevator."

Sam walked toward the elevator, puzzled by the strange man who seemed much more interested in reading his paper than helping him. Just as he got to the elevator the doors opened. No buttons, only a single slot with an identical picture of the gold card from Karen above it. Sam put it in the slot. The doors closed, and the lights dimmed to a pale gray. The elevator started moving, making a low whirring sound which got higher as the elevator increased speed. At first he thought it was going up, but then felt like it was descending, then up, then down. Sam looked up and around the elevator wondering about the strange sensation he was feeling, not sure if he were fifty stories up or down. The whirring pitch lowered as the elevator slowed, then Sam braced himself against the elevator wall as it jerked to a stop. The doors opened to a street with a green and orange bus parked at the curb. The door to the bus opened. The man with the newspaper was sitting in the driver's seat.

"Get in, Sam."

Please Sit

S am got on the bus. A forty-something woman with wire-rimmed glasses was its only passenger, sitting in the middle of the bus. She wore a plain black dress, tweed overcoat, and a black pillbox hat. She stared at Sam as he boarded the bus.

"Where's the bus going?" Sam asked the bus driver.

"She'll explain." He said as he closed the door. "Please sit."

Sam walked back toward the woman, grabbing a seat as the bus jerked forward. He sat on the bench across the aisle from the woman who never broke her gaze from him.

"Hello, Sam," the woman said in a soft voice.

"Hi." Sam waited for the woman to explain where he was going, why he was here, what was going on. She just sat and stared at Sam.

"Can you tell me what's going on?" He said.

"Yes I can," she said.

Sam waited for her to explain but she just sat there silent, staring at him. A drop of nervous sweat formed on his brow.

"Can you please tell me what's going on?"

"Yes I can." Then more silence.

"Well?" Sam asked.

"You only asked me if I could tell you what's going on. I answered that I could." Her calm voice never changing.

"Must be a lawyer," Sam thought to himself.

"I would like to know what's going on, please."

"Very well. Do you know why you're here, Sam?"

"I've got no idea." Sam looked at the driver, noticing the smile on the driver's face in the rear-view mirror as he listened to the awkward interaction.

"Sam, again, do you know why you're here?"

Sam paused for a moment to collect his thoughts. "I'm supposed to be attending an empowerment class."

"Yes you are," she said.

Sam looked outside the window. *Rebel Without A Cause starring James Dean* shone from a movie marquee. A line of men in suits and women in dresses waited to enter the theater. Next to the theater was a Studebaker dealership.

"Wait, what year is this?"

"1955."

"55? It can't be!"

"It is, Sam."

"I'm in an empowerment class in 1955?"

The woman gave Sam a slight smile, acknowledging his disbelief.

"We're almost at our first stop," she said. "I have something for you." She handed him a notebook.

"You're going to meet four people today. Each is going to talk with you about an important component of what we call Intentional Empowerment. At the end of each visit, write down the lesson you learned then come back to the bus."

Sam took the notebook, still baffled over being in the year 1955, driven around in a green and orange bus. Sam took the notebook and opened it to the first page and saw what he was to do after each lesson:

INTENTIONAL EMPOWERMENT

☐

☐

☐

☐

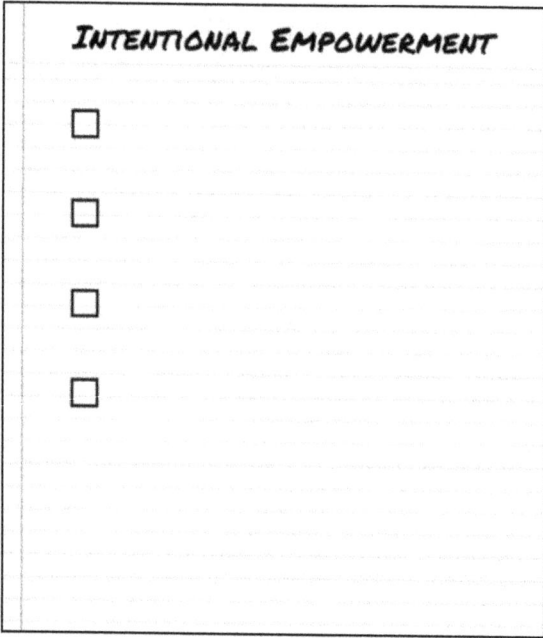

"We're here, Sam." The bus pulled up to a brick Victorian-style house with an expansive wrap-around porch supported by white columns.

"We'll be here when you're done," the woman said as the bus driver opened the door.

Sam got up from his seat, seeing the eyes of the bus driver looking at him through the rear-view mirror. Sam started walking toward the door, then turned back toward the woman.

"What's your name, ma'am."

"Rosa."

"What's your name, ma'am."

"Rosa."

Teatime

Sam stepped off the bus. The doors closed behind him and the bus sped off, leaving him in front of the Victorian house. It looked like something straight out of the 1800s except for its gold front door. He pulled the gold card from his pocket.

"Exact match," he thought as he looked at the card, then at the front door. As he climbed the steps to the house the front door opened.

"Come in, Sam."

He went into the house and found a gray-haired woman, hair pulled back in a bun, reading specs halfway down her nose, and a prominent jaw. She was sitting at a small table drinking tea.

"Would you care for some tea?" She asked.

"Yes, please." Sam looked around the room; clearly he wasn't in 1955. It looked like a bag of potpourri exploded, with all the flowered wallpaper and dainty knick-knacks. He sat down on the red velvet chair with dark walnut trim. The woman poured Sam's tea into a fine gold-rimmed cup and saucer and placed it in front of him. The woman watched him as he fumbled for his words. He took a sip of tea and started.

"I'm sorry, but can you tell me who you are?" he asked.

"Yes I can." Sam remembered this interaction from the bus and quickly changed his wording.

"Forgive me, what is your name?"

"My name is Susan Brownell Anthony. You may know me as Susan B. Anthony."

Sam nearly spat his tea back in his cup. "THE Susan B. Anthony, the very one that the nineteenth amendment is named after?"

She gave a pursed-lip smile and took a sip of tea. "Yes, but I wish they wouldn't have done that. The amendment was passed in 1920, 14 years after I died. I appreciated the recognition, but I just wanted for women to have the same voting rights as men. Then they put my face on a silver dollar in 1979 but suspended it in 1981 because it looked too much like a quarter. I suppose George W. is my doppelganger."

Sam gave her an awkward smile, not sure if he should laugh at Susan comparing her looks to Washington. He took another nervous sip of tea, trying to take in what was going on at the moment.

"Miss Anthony, I. . ."

"Please call me Susan."

"Thank you, Susan. Sorry It's not every day that I get to talk with a legend like yourself."

"How kind, Sam, I just did what I thought was the right thing to do. Is there anything you'd like to ask me before we talk about intentional empowerment?"

Sam got his bearings about him. "Can you tell me how you got involved in the suffrage movement?"

"It started when I was a teacher in Canajoharie, New York in 1848. Male teachers were paid $10 per month, and women $2.50 to do the same job. That really upset me, as you could imagine. Three years later I met Elizabeth Cady Stanton. She and I actively worked for women's rights, including the founding of the American Equal Rights Association and the National Woman Suffrage Association, where we focused on a woman's right to vote. In the 1872 presidential election, Elizabeth and I threatened to sue the registrar in Rochester, New York if he didn't register us. We succeeded in our threat and we, along with another 50 or so women, voted. I was arrested three weeks later, charged with 'criminal voting'. I continued fighting for women's suffrage until I died in 1906. I understand that equal rights is still an issue in your day."

"Unfortunately yes," Sam said.

"But enough about me. Let's talk about intentional empowerment. Do you have the notebook Rosa gave you?"

"Um, yes." Sam got out the notebook and opened to the first page.

"Very good. My job is to talk with you about the first step in intentional empowerment. Do you have any idea what it is?"

Sam put his cup down and cleared his throat to give him a few seconds to think of his answer.

"Identification of a task?" Sam's statement sounded more like a question, underscoring the fact that he was unsure of the answer she was looking for.

"Not quite, Sam. Many leaders think that empowerment means the delegation of a task, treating the person being delegated to like a dog playing fetch. The leader throws the delegation bone, the follower fetches the bone, returns it back to the leader, then waits for the next task to be delegated. The problem with this approach is the follower is only entrusted with successful completion of a task, not solving a problem. Intentional empowerment starts with entrusting a follower with a problem to solve, then ensuring the follower understands why the problem is important to solve and knows that she is accountable to solve the problem."

Sam put down his cup, intrigued by what Susan just said. "Can you give me an example?"

Susan took a quick sip of tea. "Certainly. The primary focus of the suffrage movement was to enable women to vote. This was a clear problem of which I took ownership. I knew what the goal was, I was passionate about it, and knew that I needed to own it. Now imagine if someone had said to me, 'Your job is to organize a suffrage rally.' The rallies were certainly important and necessary, but if my job were only to organize a suffrage rally without owning the problem of fighting for women to vote, I would be like the dog fetching the bone. Organize the rally, then wait for the next instruction. That is not nearly as motivating or energizing as solving the women's vote problem."

"I understand what you're saying, but not everything that needs to get done is a huge problem. Sometimes tasks just need to be worked."

Susan put her cup down and leaned toward Sam. "It is true not everything is a huge problem, but the size of the problem has nothing to do with empowerment. What matters most is that you start with a problem to solve, regardless of its size, and entrust someone to solve the problem."

"But what if the person doesn't have the skill or experience to solve the problem?"

"This is where your leadership judgment comes in. You need to balance problems with the follower's skill and experience levels to help them grow through the experience, while not setting them up for failure because it's too far outside their skill or experience level. This is where advice from your manager will help you make good decisions."

Sam thought for a moment about what Susan was saying. He could see how entrusting someone with a problem to solve was so much more meaningful than delegating a task.

"This will take a lot of practice on my part, to be conscious about expressing things that need to get done in terms of solving a problem."

"Yes it will," Susan said. "You're one in a very long line of great leaders who have to practice techniques like this. Recognizing that you need to do it is a big first step."

Susan set her cup and saucer on the table. "I believe your bus is here. Do you have something to write in your notebook?"

"Yes, thank you." He wrote the first lesson:

> ## INTENTIONAL EMPOWERMENT
>
> - ☑ ENTRUST WITH A PROBLEM TO SOLVE
> - ☐
> - ☐
> - ☐

"Thank you for your time, Susan. It's been a pleasure."

"Enjoy your journey, Sam." Sam got up and headed to the front door. He turned back to her as he opened the door.

"It's been an honor," Sam said.

Susan picked up her cup and gave him a nod. He watched her take another sip of tea as he closed the door behind him.

Mind Reader

The bus was waiting for Sam as he walked down the porch steps. He got on and sat in his same seat across from Rosa.

"How was your visit, Sam?"

Sam sat for a moment, then gave a breathless response.

"It was Susan B. Anthony."

Rosa smiled. "Yes I know. She is an amazing woman who altered the course of democracy in the United States. We only have a few minutes until our next stop. What did you learn?"

"That she died 14 years before the nineteenth amendment was passed."

"Very good, but what did you learn about intentional empowerment."

"Oh yeah, right." Sam opened his notebook and read what he wrote. "Entrust with a problem to solve."

"What does that mean to you?" Rosa asked.

Sam took a moment to gather his thoughts.

"It means that for followers to feel empowered, they need to understand why it's important to solve the problem and that they own solving it, not just having a task delegated to them."

"Are you a delegator?"

Sam squirmed at the question.

"I think so."

"You think so?"

"Um, I mean yes, I am."

Rosa's voice remained calm and measured, even though she was putting Sam on the hot seat.

"What are you going to do differently?" she asked.

"Express things that need to be done in the form of a problem to be solved, articulate why solving the problem is important, and ensure followers clearly understand the problem and their accountability in solving it."

"And what are you going to do if you're not sure how to express what needs to be done as a problem?"

"It's as if Rosa had been in the room with Susan B. Anthony, listening to the conversation," Sam thought to himself.

"No, I wasn't in the room with you." Rosa said.

"Great, she can read minds too!" He thought.

"Yes, I can, so please be honest with me. Now back to my question; what are you going to do if you are not sure about expressing what needs to be done as a problem?"

Sam took a deep breath. "Ask Karen for help."

"Very good."

Sam gave a sigh of relief at passing Rosa's pop quiz.

"We're here. See you when you're done." The bus pulled up to a simple log cabin. A single step led up to a wooden porch with the familiar gold door leading into the cabin. Sam was able to see into a dimly lit room through a window next to the door.

The bus driver opened the door. Sam stepped off the bus, climbed the steps up to the porch and knocked on the door.

"Come in, Sam."

Rail Splitter

Sam opened the gold door into the log cabin. Three candles and a fire provided the only light to the dark room. A tall, lanky man sat in a rocking chair. Hanging on the wall behind him was an axe along with a portrait of himself sitting in a chair surrounded by a woman and three boys. A small portrait of a toddler hung beneath the larger portrait.

"Please sit, Sam." The man said as he pulled another rocking chair over next to his. As the man moved closer to one of the candles Sam saw his face--thin, rugged, with a slightly bushy beard.

"Thank you, sir." Sam sat in the rocking chair as the man sat down across from him.

"Please call me Abe."

Sam was about to rock back in the chair when he stopped cold. "Mr. President?"

"Just Abe."

Sam just stared at Abe. He'd admired him ever since learning about him in elementary school--how he came from humble beginnings in Kentucky, was largely self-taught, and his ascent from an Illinois politician to the most powerful office in the United States. And here he was, sitting right across from him, gently rocking, with a smile on his face.

"Mr. er, Abe, I don't even know where to start."

"How about I explain some things about the cabin?" Abe could have read the ingredients in a can of split pea soup and Sam would have still been captivated.

"Certainly, Abe."

"I was born in this cabin in Hodgenville, Kentucky. I had an older sister Sarah and my younger brother Thomas died in infancy. Growing up I had a particular talent for wielding an axe, where I earned the nickname The Rail Splitter. And no, I did not kill vampires as Hollywood likes to say. Then again I don't really go to the theater much anymore."

Abe laughed at his joke; Sam gave an awkward smile at Lincoln joking about his own assassination.

"Oh, I'm sorry, would you like some coffee?" Abe asked.

"Yes, please."

Abe took a coffee pot from the fire, poured it into two cups, and handed one to Sam.

"Thank you."

Abe took a sip of the coffee.

"Ahhh, my favorite drink. Now about the portraits." Abe pointed to the larger portrait. "That's me sitting in the chair, my wife Mary Todd, and my sons Willie, Tad, and Robert. The smaller portrait is of my son Edward Baker. Edward died a month before his fourth birthday. Willie died when he was 11, and Tad died when he was 18. Both Edward and Willie died while I was still alive, and Tad died six years after my assassination. Poor Mary had to bury not only me but three of her sons."

"I'm so sorry, sir."

"Thank you. I can't fathom how difficult it was for Mary. She was such a saint. But enough about me, let's talk about you."

Sam felt so strange talking about himself with the man he considered a hero all his life, but he also knew the why he was there in the first place.

"Yes, Abe, as much as I'd love to talk about a million other things, I'm supposed to talk with you about empowerment."

"Ah yes, intentional empowerment. I expect you already talked with Susan about entrusting a follower with a problem to solve?"

"Yes, sir."

"Good. The second step in intentional empowerment is the articulation of guiding principles."

"Guiding principles, sir?"

"Yes, guiding principles. You may also think of them as rules, requirements or guidelines. Those things the follower needs to adhere to in solving the problem you've entrusted."

Sam took a sip of coffee and leaned forward in the rocker, hanging on Abe's every word. Abe continued.

"I'll give you an example of a guiding principle. In 1862, Horace Greeley, the editor of the New York Tribune, penned an open letter to me, asking me to enforce the confiscation acts that were enacted in 1861 and 1862 to liberate slaves in seceded states. I wrote a letter back to him." Abe pulled a piece of paper from his pocket and read.

"My paramount object in this struggle is to save the Union, and is not either to save or to destroy slavery. If I could save the Union without freeing any slave I would do it, and if I could save it by freeing all slaves I would do it; and if I could save it by freeing some and leaving others alone I would also do that." Abe folded the paper and put it back in his pocket.

"My guiding principle during the civil war was to prevent the breakup of the Union, and I was willing to do so regardless of slavery's fate. I personally wanted slavery abolished but was willing to keep it in whole or part if it meant preserving the Union."

Abe took another sip of coffee, closing his eyes as it trickled down his throat. He continued. "Now as it relates to intentional empowerment, followers need to know what they can and cannot do to solve their problems. This isn't about telling followers *how* to do something, it's about providing information that will help them make decisions about how they solve the problem. Let me give you another example."

Abe pointed to the axe hanging on the wall. "Let's say I decide to go into the axe business, but I don't want to manufacture the handles. I entrust you with the problem of finding a reliable supplier to make axe handles for my business. As guiding principles, I tell you that the supplier must be able to manufacture a thousand handles a month, a handle must support a two-pound axe head, and that the axe handles must be made of hickory, ash, walnut, or birch. Notice I don't tell you *how* to go about finding the supplier; I give you enough information so you can figure out how to find the best supplier for my axe business. The guiding principles help you solve the problem. Does this make sense?"

"Completely," Sam said. "I can think of several situations in the past year when I delegated something to one of my folks but didn't give them enough information about what they could and couldn't do. In each situation, I had the person go back and rework something that was clear to me, but not at all obvious to them. I blamed them for not thinking for themselves when in reality it was probably about my lack of clarity in my guiding principles."

"Well done," Abe said. I think our time is about up. Do you have something to write in your notebook?"

"I do." Sam opened the notebook and wrote the second step:

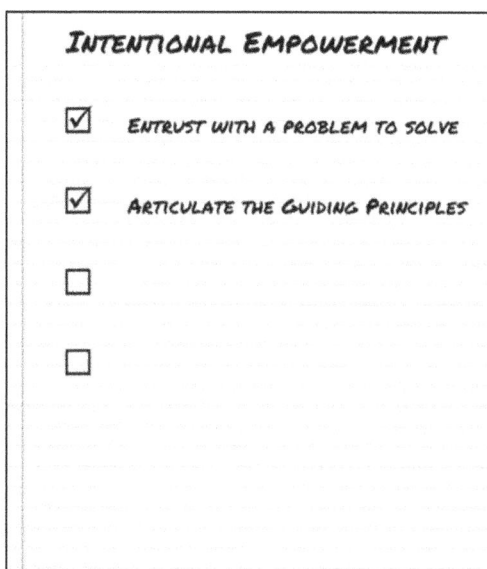

INTENTIONAL EMPOWERMENT

☑ ENTRUST WITH A PROBLEM TO SOLVE

☑ ARTICULATE THE GUIDING PRINCIPLES

☐

☐

"It's been a pleasure talking with you, Sam." Abe got up from his chair and took Sam's coffee cup. "My best to you in your journey."

"Thank you, Mr. President. It has truly been an honor speaking with you." Sam got up and shook

Abe's hand. Abe gave a fatherly smile and nod, leading Sam to the door.

"Be well, Sam." As he walked out the door, the bus pulled up to the house. He looked back and saw Abe's silhouette through the cabin window, sitting back in his rocking chair, cup of coffee in hand, looking up at the portraits.

Sushi

He boarded the bus to see Rosa in her same seat, eating sushi with chopsticks. Sam sat in his same seat, watching as she put a dab of wasabi sauce on her roll, dipped it in soy sauce, and put it in her mouth. Her eyes closed as she slowly chewed the rice, seaweed, and salmon delicacy.

"I only wish this was popular when I was alive, I would have eaten it every day." She wiped her mouth and put her dish on the seat next to her. "I'll finish this later; tell me what you learned."

Sam stared at the half-eaten sushi roll on the seat. The smell of it alone made him want to retch. He looked back up at Rosa, who was staring at him waiting for his response.

"Yes, it was President Lincoln, he wanted me to call him Abe. He was my childhood hero. I could have sat there all day listening to him."

"Good, now can you tell me what you learned?"

"Oh yes, sorry." Sam opened the notebook. "I learned about articulating guiding principles."

"And what about guiding principles did you learn?" she asked.

"Guiding principles are also known as rules or requirements that followers need to adhere to in solving their problems."

"Good, what else?"

Sam thought back to the discussion, realizing that Rosa was looking for the correct answer to her question.

"I learned that guiding principles aren't about telling the follower *how* to do something, it's about providing enough clarity and guidelines so the follower can decide the best way to solve the problem."

"Correct," she said as she picked up another piece of sushi roll and popped it in her mouth.

"Can you see how you might do things differently as a result of what Abe told you?"

"Definitely. In the past I either didn't provide enough information to help a follower get something done or I would get overly prescriptive in wanting the follower to do something the way I would do it. I took a "my way or the highway" approach to getting things done, which is not only disempowering, but frustrating to the follower."

"Well done, Sam. We're almost at the next stop, you should get ready to go."

"Wait Rosa, can you tell me more about you?"

"There's no time right now, Sam. We'll talk later."

The bus pulled up to an ornate white building with detailed carvings. The walkway leading to the building from the sidewalk was white stone. At its end was the familiar gold door Sam saw on the other buildings. Sam got up to leave as Rosa picked up her plate of sushi. He walked along the stone walkway up to the gold door and knocked.

"Enter!" said a gruff voice in a thick French accent.

Le Petit Caporal

S am walked through the gold door to what looked like an expansive palace, with sculpted molding and ornate, colorful scenery painted on the walls. A massive chandelier hung in the center of the room.

"Funny, it doesn't look nearly this big from the street," Sam thought to himself.

"You call me small?" a man approached him, dressed in an eighteenth century French military uniform with white leggings, navy coat, and a chest full of medals.

"Great, another mind reader," Sam thought. The man gave Sam a steely gaze.

"You Americans, you all think I'm this tiny man, even naming a complex after me. Did you know I was, how you say in English, 5 foot 7? Three inches taller than the average Frenchman in my day, Alexander the Great and Mussolini were my height, Stalin only an inch taller, Lenin was 5 foot 5, and Khrushchev was 5 foot 3. But it's me they called *Le Petit Caporal!*"

"Napoleon?" Sam asked.

"General Napoleon Bonaparte to you, sir."

"Sorry, General."

"Over here." Napoleon led them to a small gold table with gold chairs upholstered in deep purple fabric.

"Now, you here to talk about intentional empowerment, no?

"Yes."

"Take out your notebook and listen good."

His abruptness was in stark contrast to the calming demeanors of Rosa, Susan, and Abe; though Sam found the general amusing.

"You already heard about entrusting with a problem and guiding principles, no?"

"Yes."

"Now here is third step, agree upon key dates. Do you know why important?"

"I think so, I mean . . . "

"Enough! I tell you." Napoleon sat on the end of his seat, leaning forward, gaze locked, as if challenging Sam to a staring contest. "During times of war my field generals and I strategize regularly about dates;

when to attack, when to expect supplies, when to stand down. If someone didn't understand or ignored a date for when he needed to do something, then other people died. With intentional empowerment, understanding of key dates is crucial, but hopefully without people dying."

Napoleon paused. Sam sat waiting for him to continue.

"That was a joke, you think funny, no?"

"You mean about people dying?" Sam asked.

"You Americans don't know funny. I continue."

"Uh, okay." Sam said.

"Now back to dates. When you empower a follower to solve a problem, both you and follower need to have same view of important dates. Those dates could be about when problem needs to be solved, when an approach needs to be reviewed with other stakeholder, or other date that is important to solving the problem. You want to hear example where this go bad?"

Sam was about to open his mouth before Napoleon interrupted.

"I tell you anyway. You know I created Napoleonic Code, right? Many say my greatest achievement. It defined laws about people, property, and civil procedure that was basis for laws in many other countries. Even your state of Louisiana has some laws influenced by my Code. I no want to sell Louisiana to you Americans but I needed the money. You got steal for 68 million francs. You like Louisiana, no?"

"Yes a steal at 15 million dollars. Great gumbo," Sam said.

"Idiot! Gumbo not French! *Mon dieu*."

"Very sorry, General."

"I continue." Napoleon took a deep breath to compose himself. "Before my Code become law in 1805, France tried rewriting laws many times. Once in 1793, Jean-Jacques Régis de Cambacérès was given one month to draft new laws. It fail badly. He was given impossible date that he not agree to. The results were disaster. He later work with me on Napoleonic Code, and it enacted in 1804."

Sam was fascinated. "I wish I would have paid better attention to history in school," he said.

"I tell you more. I fought 60 battles, lost only eight. What battle you know me for?"

"Um, Waterloo?"

"Yes!" Napoleon's face turned beet-red.

"After my first exile to Island of Elba in 1814, I escape after eight months and regain control of France. I then fight British and Prussians at Waterloo in June 1815 and was defeated bad. They exiled me to Saint Helena Island in South Atlantic where I stay until I die in 1821. The phrase *met his waterloo* is--what you call it--slang for experiencing a final defeat. That what people know me for. *Imbéciles!*"

"Napoleon, we talked about this; be nice." The two heard Rosa's voice. Napoleon looked around, searching for her in the room. "Okay, I sorry," he said. He leaned forward to Sam and whispered, "She not here. I forget she can hear me, I not want third exile."

Sam smiled, amused at this funny little man. He continued. "General, I understand the idea of a date when a problem needs to be solved by, but sometimes that isn't always known early on. What then?"

"Yes I call that *a date for a date*. The follower may need to take time to understand work before can agree to completion date; they should provide a date that they will know when next phase of work will be done. Then as the follower learns more, they get more precise with future dates."

"But what if something must be done by a certain date and the follower just needs to make it happen?" Sam asked.

"Yes, sometimes dates are fixed. That's where scope and budget important. If the leader mandates a completion date, then he should be flexible on scope of work and budget that is given to the follower to solve the problem."

"So agreement on key dates isn't only about dates, it's about budget and scope too?"

"Yes. If a leader is going to fix dates, then must be flexible on scope and budget. Constrain all three and problem might not get solved in timeframe you want."

"Dates, scope, and budget--check."

"But now we talk about what I refer to as the fine wine dilemma. The best wines, French of course, can take years to go from vine to glass, but you want same quality French wine in a month. No amount of money or resources will reduce time to make fine wine down to a month. Same thing with solving problem. There comes a point where more money or less scope no make a difference to a due date. Some leaders get stuck in a 'just throw people at problem' to try to meet a date. You could get to a point where additional resources have reverse effect on a date because too many cooks in kitchen, so to speak."

"How do you know when you can't do something any faster?" Sam asked.

"First, make sure the date is truly a must-have date and not about leader being impatient. Second, listen to the problem owner. He or she will tell you if date is impossible. Third, use a coach to help confirm work and explore what could be changed to meet a date. *Comprendre*?"

"I do." Sam collected his thoughts before explaining further. "And I realize now how much I did wrong as a leader. I either was vague on date expectations, assigned unrealistic dates that my folks didn't agree with, or didn't equip them with enough budget or scope flexibility to get the work done. Yet most of the time they just saluted me with a 'Yes, sir' and marched into battle knowing that they were destined for failure."

"I like military analogy," Napoleon said. Do you have something you need to write in your notebook?"

"Yes."

INTENTIONAL EMPOWERMENT

☑ ENTRUST WITH A PROBLEM TO SOLVE

☑ ARTICULATE THE GUIDING PRINCIPLES

☑ AGREE UPON KEY DATES

☐

"Well done, soldier. Before you leave I give you something."

Napoleon pulled from his coat and gave Sam a wooden plaque, on it was a gold plate with the engraved phrase:

La seule façon de diriger les gens est de leur montrer un avenir: un leader est un concessionnaire dans l'espoir.

"Thank you, what does it mean?"

"It means, *The only way to lead people is to show them a future: a leader is a dealer in hope.* It one of my best quotes, you like?"

Sam took the plaque, brushing his fingers over the engraved words. "I don't know how to thank you enough, General. This means so much to me."

"You cannot thank me enough. Your bus will be here soon. Carry on."

"Thank you, General." Napoleon got up from the chair and led Sam out. "He looks more like 5 foot 4," Sam thought as he walked out the door.

"I'm 5 foot 7!" Sam heard as the gold door slammed shut.

Man on the Bus

The bus was already waiting outside of Napoleon's palace. Sam boarded the bus, but there was a man wearing a gray suit and a fedora sitting in the place where Rosa had sat.

"Where's Rosa?" Sam asked the bus driver.

He just pointed, directing Sam to sit down. Sam walked back and sat next to the man.

"Where's Rosa?"

"Do you know who you've been sitting next to all this time? She was born Rosa Louise McCauley. At 19 she married Raymond Parks. You've been sitting next to Rosa Parks."

"Wow! Rosa Parks. I've always admired her courage in not giving in to the bus driver who tried to make her give up her seat to a white man. Why didn't she tell me who she was?"

"Rosa takes her responsibility to teach leaders about intentional empowerment very seriously. She wanted to make sure you were almost done with the class before you knew about her. She doesn't like to talk about herself, which is why I'm here."

"Okay, then who are you?"

"I'm the man that Rosa was supposed to give up her seat to. And the bus driver who has been driving you around, his name is James Blake. He was the Montgomery, Alabama bus driver who, on December 1, 1955, told four black passengers to get up and make room for four white passengers to sit. Three of them got up, but Rosa wouldn't move. Rosa was arrested and on December 5 was found guilty of violating segregation laws and fined $14. Afterward she was harassed so much that she, her husband and her mother moved from Montgomery to Detroit. Long story short, Rosa helped initiate the civil rights movement and was a recognized symbol of strength in the fight to end racial segregation."

Sam was transfixed with the man's words. "I'd read about Rosa in school but never really comprehended the courage she showed not only in not giving up her seat but in her being a continued activist to end segregation. How did the three of you end up working together on the intentional empowerment class?"

"Rosa will explain that more at the end of the class. What did you learn from General Bonaparte?"

"Oh yes, sure." Sam opened up his notebook. "I learned that the third step in intentional empowerment is to agree upon key dates. That agreement doesn't mean being dictatorial about a date, but being pragmatic about what a follower needs to get something done, how budget and scope influence a date's achievability, how getting *a date for a date* gives a follower time to figure out how he or she wants to attack a problem, and that throwing more resources at a problem doesn't necessarily help things get done faster."

"Well done. I see he gave you his plaque on giving people hope. Did he go through his "heights of famous world leaders" speech?"

"He did."

The man laughed. "He's done that with all of us."

"He appears to have a Napoleon Complex," Sam said. "Look, here's your last stop." The bus pulled up to a caboose parked on a railroad track.

"Will I see you again, sir?" Sam asked.

"Possibly. Best of luck to you, Sam."

"And to you." Sam shook the man's hand, got up, and left the bus. He walked to the back of the caboose where he stepped up the three stairs to the gold door.

"All aboard, Sam," he heard as he opened the door.

Narcolepsy

S am stepped into the caboose, barren except for two wooden boxes. An older woman wearing a head scarf and simple wool coat sat on one of the boxes.

"Please sit down, Sam." The woman pointed to the other wooden box. Sam did as he was told.

"Who are you?" Sam asked.

"I was born Araminta Ross on a slavery plantation in Dorchester County, Maryland in 1820. I later changed my first name to my mother's name, Harriet. When I was 25, I married a free black man named John Tubman. You probably know me as Harriet Tubman."

"Mrs. Tubman, what an honor."

"Please, it's just Harriet. I just don't like hearing the last name. My marriage was not good, and my husband tried to sell me and my two brothers farther south, so I left him and Maryland and escaped to Philadelphia where I worked as a housekeeper. I was a free woman, but so many family and friends left behind were still enslaved. I ended up going south 19 times to transport slaves up to freedom in Canada. On the third trip I planned to take my husband north, but he had since remarried after I escaped and wanted to stay in Maryland."

"Why did you take them all the way to Canada?" Sam shifted from one butt cheek to the other on the hard wooden box.

"Good question. The Fugitive Slave Act of 1850 allowed fugitive and free slaves in the north to be captured and enslaved. Slaves were no longer safe in the north, so the only way to ensure their safety was to take them to Canada."

"And you did this 19 times?"

"Yes, I lost count on the number of people we transported, but even if it was only one life freed then it all was worth it, despite the $40,000 reward put on my head if I were captured."

Sam prepared to ask Harriet another question but noticed she had fallen fast asleep.

"Harriet?" Sam nudged her. "Harriet?"

Harriet rustled and opened her eyes.

"Did I fall asleep? I'm so sorry. When I was 12, I saw an overseer about to throw a heavy weight at a fugitive slave. I stepped in front of the slave and the weight struck me in the head. I've suffered from headaches and narcolepsy ever since. If it happens again, just nudge me. I should come to pretty quickly."

"Certainly, Harriet."

"Now let's get to work. You're here to learn about the fourth step to intentional empowerment, right?"

"Yes."

"Actually this step is probably the easiest to do but is the most overlooked. The step is to establish a follow-up cadence."

"Follow-up cadence, can you explain?" Sam asked.

"Certainly. Something I learned from those 19 runs was that slaves were relying on me to continue returning south. Had I not followed through on my commitment, those still enslaved would have stayed slaves or, even worse, lost their lives. They had an expectation of me, and my job was to meet the expectation to help slaves obtain their freedom."

"Harriet, can you help me with how expectations relate to a follow-up cadence?"

"Good question, Sam. Establishing a follow-up cadence is all about establishing, maintaining and, when necessary, resetting expectations. While the problem is being worked the leader and follower need to stay aligned on the problem, key dates, needed resources and any unanticipated issues where the follower needs the leader's help. To ensure things like this are discussed, a periodic meeting helps everyone stay aligned and ensures any changes in expectations are discussed."

"So you're talking about a team meeting, right?" Sam didn't like where this was going. He saw meetings as a waste of time because "real work" wasn't getting done.

"It could be a team meeting, but what I'm thinking about is something a bit more focused between the leader and the follower, where they can have a candid discussion about progress, any barriers, or advice the follower would like from the leader."

Sam shifted butt cheeks to get more comfortable.

"I like the focused discussion. We use a lot of tools that can help that like email, phone calls, and video in the event that face-to-face doesn't work. I suppose those could be used to facilitate the discussion."

"I'm not sure what those things are, but if you think helpful, then certainly," Harriet said.

"Oh, sorry about the lingo. I understand the discussion part, but what's the frequency?"

"That's totally up to the leader and follower. Things that influence frequency include the severity of the problem, the experience level of the follower, and the likelihood that the follower will encounter difficulties. Great leaders don't employ a one-size-fits-all approach to a follow-up cadence. They look at the circumstances then recommend a cadence frequency appropriate for the situation. I've seen them as frequently as multiple times a day for highly critical and time-sensitive problems, all the way to monthly or beyond. What's important is to assess the work, then agree on an appropriate cadence."

This was almost like a foreign language to Sam. He never considered any kind of planned follow-up cadence with his followers, let alone something that was right-sized based on the situation.

"I get the need for focused meetings and an agreed-upon cadence frequency, but how about meeting duration?"

Harriet leaned forward and stared into Sam's eyes. "As short as possible."

"Really? I always despised meetings because I thought they were just a bunch of people blathering about nothing when I had other things to do. You're telling me to make my follow-ups as short as possible?"

"That's exactly what I'm saying," Harriet said.

"That's music to my ears; if it were up to me, I'd make them five minutes."

"Slow down, Sam. There may be a bit of trial and error on this. If you see that you're not covering the most important things in the time allotted, then the leader and follower need to assess whether to add more time or adjust what is covered in the meeting. As you get more experience, you'll get a better feel for not just meeting duration, but rhythm and whether you use tools like that, what did you say, email? Allow yourself to break some eggs as you figure this out."

Sam did one last shuffle on the wooden box.

"Sam, does all of this make sense?"

"It does, and I'm embarrassed about how poorly I've done this in the past. My follow-up cadence was all about managing to a crisis, where some big issue threatened work, which meant everyone working late nights to get things done. It was never deliberate and planned. I just accepted that was part of the job and expected my folks to feel the same. What I now realize is that a well-executed follow-up cadence can help me avoid a lot of the fire drills that I've accepted as a necessary evil. You're right, it's a simple thing that just requires a little discipline."

"Well said, Sam. I believe you have something to write in your notebook?"

"I do."

```
┌─────────────────────────────────────────┐
│                                          │
│   INTENTIONAL EMPOWERMENT                │
│                                          │
│   ☑   ENTRUST WITH A PROBLEM TO SOLVE    │
│                                          │
│   ☑   ARTICULATE THE GUIDING PRINCIPLES  │
│                                          │
│   ☑   AGREE UPON KEY DATES               │
│                                          │
│   ☑   ESTABLISH A FOLLOW-UP CADENCE      │
│                                          │
│                                          │
└─────────────────────────────────────────┘
```

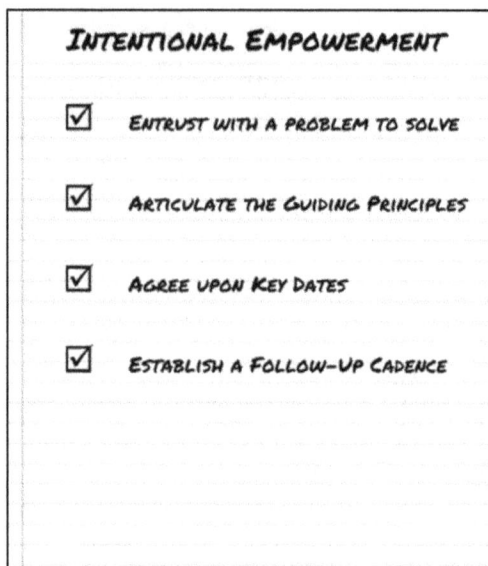

"Your bus should be just outside, Sam. Best to you."

"Thank you for everything, Harriet." Sam got up, turned and walked toward the gold door.

"Enjoy the journey," Harriet said as Sam opened the door and ran down the caboose stairs.

"I will," Sam thought, expecting that Harriet could too read his thoughts.

All

T he bus was waiting as Sam descended the caboose steps. The door was already open, but James the bus driver wasn't in his seat.

Sam boarded the bus. Rosa, the bus driver, and the man who wanted to sit in Rosa's seat were all sitting in a row. Behind them was a "Colored" sign with "All" spray-painted over it.

"Come sit, Sam." Rosa said.

Sam sat in the seat in front of the three, his back to the window, his eyes fixed on the spray-painted sign right above the passengers.

"How was your visit with Harriet?" Rosa asked.

"Amazing, like all my visits today."

"What did you learn?"

"I learned how bad I am at follow-up. Harriet gave me great advice about creating a structured follow-up cadence to keep a leader and follower aligned through problem resolution. I learned that the follow-up frequency and delivery mechanism can flex based on need, and that meetings should be as short as possible. But most importantly, the follow-up cadence requires discipline. It was a real eye-opener for me."

"Very good, Sam," Rosa said. "Harriet was the model of discipline, with her 19 underground railroad trips from the south to Canada, enabling scores of fugitive slaves to start a new life of freedom."

"Yes, amazing lady. But Rosa, why didn't you tell me who you were?"

"How would that have helped in your intentional empowerment journey?" She asked.

Sam was caught off-guard by the question. "But, you're Rosa Parks! You're an icon in the civil rights movement!" He looked up at the spray-painted sign. "It's you who defied these two guys and spearheaded the end of segregation. Don't you understand the impact you had?"

"We all three played a role in shaping history, as did Susan, Abe, Napoleon, and Harriet. We are all dead now, our time passed. Our job now is to inspire the next generation of leaders, and we all agree that intentional empowerment is a vital skill that leaders must master. We want to pay it forward, as the saying goes, to the next generation. Drawing on our accomplishments while we were alive is now an effective tool in getting a young leader's attention. Do you think listening to a boring lecturer would have had the same impact?"

"Definitely not," Sam said.

"There you have it. I expect you'll remember the day and the lessons you learned better than sitting in a sterile classroom."

James and the man sat quietly as Rosa spoke, giving an occasional affirming nod.

"I do have a couple of questions, though." Sam said.

"Certainly."

"Where did the gold card come from?"

"The card gets passed down from leader to leader. Your manager Karen got the card five years ago from her manager. She sat in the very same place you did at the end of her intentional empowerment class and asked the same question. I explained to her that she could give the card to one leader who she saw great potential but needed help with empowering followers. She decided to give the card to you."

"Can I give it back to her so she can give it to someone else?"

"No. That responsibility lies with you. It's now up to you to decide when to use the card and who to give it to. It could be in a day, a month, or years from now."

"But how will I know who to give it to?" Sam asked.

"That's for you to figure out, Sam. Just don't be in a rush to do it. You'll know when it's right."

"I'm not sure about this, but I'll trust you."

"It's time for you to go, Sam. We wish you the best in your intentional empowerment journey."

They all got up and Sam shook each of their hands. He walked to the front of the bus, gave one last look to the three, and started down the bus steps, seeing the elevator with the gold doors. He stepped off the bus just as the elevator doors opened. He entered the elevator, turned, and took one last look at the bus, its door closing just as the elevator doors shut. The elevator began its strange journey, the whirring sound rising in pitch, the lights dimming, then the jerk as it came to a stop. The doors opened to the stark white room with marble floors. James was sitting in the folding chair, reading his newspaper. Sam exited the elevator.

"Goodbye James."

James looked up from his newspaper, winked at Sam, and resumed reading.

Sam walked out of the building and looked at his watch. "Five after eight. That whole thing only took five minutes?" he said. "Incredible."

French Pastries

S am spent the day walking around the city, thinking about the discussions he had, periodically looking at the notebook with its four steps.

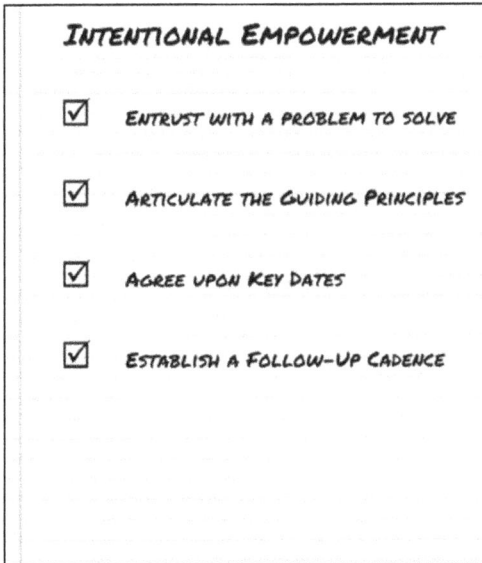

INTENTIONAL EMPOWERMENT

☑ ENTRUST WITH A PROBLEM TO SOLVE

☑ ARTICULATE THE GUIDING PRINCIPLES

☑ AGREE UPON KEY DATES

☑ ESTABLISH A FOLLOW-UP CADENCE

He thought about Susan's wise advice about defining a problem to solve in that potpourri room. Abe enjoying his cup of coffee as he talked about guiding principles. Napoleon's height comparisons as he described key dates. And the wood boxes in Harriet's caboose as she spoke of a follow-up cadence. And Rosa's love of sushi and how she explained his responsibility to pay the class forward to another leader with great potential. There were so many more questions he wanted to ask each of them about their life experiences, their struggles, their dreams, their fears. He decided to go back to 18 Claire Place to talk more with them. As he approached the address, he caught a whiff of hot bread as he looked in the window at the French pastries in the exact spot where the gold door was just hours earlier.

"Hmm," Sam said as he smiled and walked past.

Next Performance Appraisal

Sam waited outside Karen's office. A year ago, Sam was filled with angst over the critical feedback on his employee satisfaction survey.

"Come in, Sam," Karen said as she motioned him in.

"Good morning," Sam said.

"Yes, it is."

Sam put his water bottle and folder down on the table and sat. His performance appraisal was already on the table. Karen walked over and sat across from him.

"Sam let's talk about your performance over the past year—both strengths and areas for improvement. First, strengths."

Sam smiled as she began.

"Great delivery results. You come in on budget, customer satisfaction exceeds expectations. Nice work, just like last year."

"Thank you, Karen."

"Now let's talk about your employee satisfaction survey results. Last year you were at the fifth percentile; this year you're at the ninetieth percentile. Outstanding progress. Let's talk about why."

"Certainly," Sam said. "It started with the intentional empowerment class you sent me to. Susan B. Anthony really helped me to understand the importance of entrusting a follower with a problem to solve, and how simply delegating a task wasn't enough to motivate someone to great performance. Then Abraham Lincoln articulated how guiding principles helped me to think through and communicate the guidelines and requirements a follower needs to adhere to in solving the problem. Then there's Napoleon."

"He's an interesting character," Karen said.

Sam chuckled. "Boy, is he! His focus on agreeing upon key dates and how budget, scope and schedule all work together to help a follower deliver results was something I never really understood until he so bluntly explained it. Then Harriet Tubman talked about how crucial a follow-up cadence is to managing expectations and keeping me and a follower aligned on work. It also really brought home for me how integral it is to be responsive to any issues the follower is dealing with. Without a follow-up cadence, timely issue resolution is impossible."

"Very good, Sam."

"Oh, and then Rosa Parks was so good at reinforcing each of the intentional empowerment steps and making sure I really understood what Susan, Abe, Napoleon, and Harriet were trying to teach me."

"Was it difficult applying what you learned after the class?"

Sam leaned forward; palms face down on the table. "Very."

"How so?"

"For the first few months I kept forgetting about the intentional empowerment steps and found myself drifting back into old habits. I was very open with my team that I was working on learning intentional empowerment and asked each of them to call me out when I wasn't using it. There were a number of times where team members candidly reminded me how I was delegating tasks versus entrusting problems, not giving good guiding principles, being vague on dates, or not being available when problems came up. It took me a long time to make intentional empowerment a habit, and to get to the place where I did it without having to think about it. Having my team hold me accountable and being patient with myself were both paramount in changing my ways."

Karen took a sip of coffee. "Sam, let me tell you something. What you've just said is nearly identical to what I told my manager years back when I went to the intentional empowerment class. Changes like this take time. I was very frustrated with myself in not developing new habits quickly enough, but my manager counseled me to keep at it. I did, and it paid off for me, and now it's paid off for you."

"It has. Having visual cues in my office has also helped. I framed the intentional empowerment steps and hung them on my wall, next to the plaque Napoleon gave me."

"Good technique, Sam." Karen and Sam talked through the rest of his performance appraisal and what he needed to do to continue his professional growth.

"You'll be sitting in my chair someday," Karen said as they wrapped up their discussion.

"Thank you, Karen," Sam said as he left her office.

Karen went back to her desk. She opened the bottom drawer and pulled out a wooden plaque. She took a sip of coffee as she read the French phrase on the plaque's gold plate.

Five Years Later

Tracy sat outside Sam's office, dreading the discussion she was about to have.

"Come in, Tracy," Sam said.

"Thank you." Tracy's hands shook as she sat at the table. They reviewed Tracy's performance appraisal, her employee survey results, and her needing to improve how she empowers followers. As they talked, Sam heard Rosa's words, *you'll know when it's right.* Sam got up from his chair, opened his desk drawer and pulled out the gold card.

Historical sources: Britannica.com, History.com, Wikipedia.com, PBS.org

See a sample chapter from *Behind Gold Doors-Nine Crucial Elements to Achieve Good-Enough Contentment*

At This Time...

Ty got his morning coffee and turned on his computer. The first email was from one of the companies where he had sent his resume. He hovered the cursor over the email, took a deep breath, and double-tapped the track pad, opening the email.

Dear Mr. Taylor:

Thank you so much for your interest in Lake Industries. At this time...

Ty closed the email without reading further. They all started out with something like *"at this time," "unfortunately,"* or *"we currently don't."* They ended with an empty *"we will keep your resume on file should something become available which matches your skillset. Thank you for your interest in blah-di-blah company."* He had gotten dozens of them, each one like a slug to the gut. Just as he shut his laptop Kate came into the kitchen. She immediately could tell what had happened.

"I'm so sorry, Ty," Kate said as she came around to him and put her hand on his shoulder. "Something will turn up; you just need to be patient."

Ty took a sip of coffee. "It's been six months and not one bite. Severance is gone, and the pittance we get from unemployment runs out next week. How much more patient do I need to be?"

"I wish I knew, honey. We're doing okay on finances and I've got plenty of client work in backlog. We've been through tougher times than this and we got through it. We'll get through this too." Kate poured herself a cup of coffee in a travel mug and took her lunch out of the fridge. "We'll talk more tonight, honey; I believe in you."

"I'm so lucky to have you," Ty said. "Do you want a lift to the train station?"

"I'll walk this morning, but how about you pick me up tonight? I should be on the 5:40, I'll call you if not."

"Got it, I love you."

Kate leaned over to kiss Ty. "Love you too."

Kate headed down the hallway to the front door. Ty heard the door open then gently click shut as she left.

His routine was the same every day. After Kate left for work, he'd finish going through his email inbox, then cruise the news websites, then up for a shower, then onto the job websites. As the weeks went by and the rejections piled up, he cast his job search net wider and wider; even looking at jobs that new college grads could do. He spent hours each day looking at opportunities, trying to network, and responding to job postings. Sometimes after lunch he would break routine and just sit on the couch with a bowl of chips watching afternoon talk shows. The couch sessions increased in frequency as he became more and more depressed. Most times he just wore sweats, since his pants had become too tight, but he knew better than to wear something with an elastic waistband if he and Kate were going out. He'd do the best he could to squeeze into his pants, preferring hooks over snaps to avoid them popping under pressure.

Socializing with friends was the worst. "How's the job search coming?" He'd hear it over and over. "Just great, pursuing a couple of opportunities," he'd lie, then try to change the topic. He particularly hated having to face his daughters and his shame of feeling like such a loser-unemployed dad.

Ty finished up his morning activities then made himself a tuna sandwich with chips and soda. "Wonder what's on TV this afternoon?" he said. "No, I need to work." He looked at his laptop, then the TV remote, then back at the laptop. "Actually, I need to get out." He finished his lunch, got his jacket and left the house for a walk.

"It's a beautiful Fall day," Ty said to himself as he walked down the street towards the train station. It was about a mile walk, one that he used to do every day when he worked at Conset, and the same that Kate did each day to get to her office. The street was lined with reddish-yellow trees that rained leaves onto the ground with each gust of wind. Ty took deep breaths as he walked, feeling the cool Autumn air fill his lungs. He walked by the park next to the train station. Two mothers with strollers sat on a bench talking. A man played fetch with his dog; on each throw the dog would run as fast as he could to the ball, kicking up a trail of leaves with each lunge. As he got closer to the train station, he noticed an old woman sitting in a wheelchair next to a bench. He slowed his walk to look at her. She wore a huge hat adorned with white flowers, a pink polka-dot sweater, and red and orange striped pants. On her lap sat a large paisley-print carpet bag. Her makeup looked as if it were applied with a putty knife. Her sunken eyes stared at Ty as he walked by, expressionless in her gaze, even though Ty smiled at her as he passed. As he continued to the station, he turned to look at the woman, who was still ogling him. Ty quickened his pace to get out of her eyeshot.

"Think I'll go into the city," Ty said to himself as he arrived at the train station. "I can make the 1:05, get into Chicago by 2, then Kate and I can ride the 5:40 back together.". He loved walking along Lakeshore Drive and experiencing the sights, smells and sounds of the expansive Lake Michigan. He bought a ticket and waited on the platform for the train to Union Station. The train's horn broke the silence of the Fall day as it approached the station; followed by the grinding of the metal wheels on the track as the train slowly approached the platform. He stood to board the train as it came to a stop. "How odd," he said to himself. The car was a familiar dingy silver, weathered by the countless trips around Chicagoland. What wasn't so typical were the doors--gleaming gold, looking as if they were just delivered from the foundry and installed that day. The doors slid open, Ty boarded, then with a whoosh the doors closed behind him. He looked up and down the empty car and sat down in the seat next to the doors. Ty pulled out his phone, waiting for the train to depart. Just then the door abruptly opened.

"Help me!" Ty heard as he turned and looked back at the door.

See a sample from *Behind Gold Doors-Seven Steps to Create a Disability Inclusive Organization*

Rain Gear

For the rest of the day Jade couldn't get Kelly's story out of her mind. She had never known anyone close to her with a disability and couldn't imagine the pain Kelly felt watching her father die the way he did.

"*How could I possibly do this justice?*" she thought to herself. "*I'm an engineer, I build stuff. I don't have the experience to do this. What if I fail? I don't want to disappoint Kelly, knowing how important this is to her.*" Jade got up to get some water. On the way she looked outside at the dark clouds forming. "*Gonna need the rain gear tonight,*" she thought.

At 5:30 p.m. she packed up her stuff, slipped on her rain pants and jacket, and headed out. She walked by Kelly's office just as Kelly looked up and gave Jade a quick wave goodbye.

It was unusually dark for this time of year. The rain quickly went from a light mist to a torrential downpour. Jade had ridden in rain before, but nothing quite like this. "*Just go slow,*" she thought as she went through each intersection. She considered stopping and waiting it out, but there was no guarantee that it would let up. "*Halfway home. I can do this.*"

Then it happened.

See more at ***behindgolddoors.com***

See a sample chapter from *Why Don't They Follow Me? 12 Easy Lessons to Boost Your Leadership Skills*

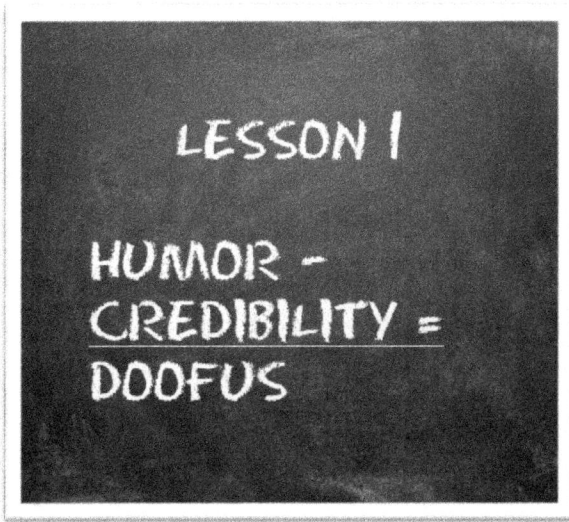

E d was just appointed team leader in a public works organization of the federal government. In preparing for his first meeting with his new team, Ed thought long and hard about some of his prior managers' leadership styles. One characteristic he par-ticularly admired in several of his managers was the ability to connect with the team through humor. He decided on a strategy that would help the team accept him as a leader—he would show his human side and use humor to connect with them.

Ed had his first meeting with the team and was very satisfied with the results. The team seemed to really like him. The meeting was filled with laughter and both the team and Ed seemed to really be enjoying themselves. Ed was very happy and believed things were getting off to a great start.

With each passing meeting, though, there seemed to be a growing concern among the team. While Ed seemed to connect with the team, he didn't see the cooperation on getting things done as he had hoped. There were also a couple of team members who asked for permission to interview for positions outside of the group. Ed was growing concerned over the trend and asked Betty, one of the team members, what she thought was the problem. Betty's counsel hit Ed right between the eyes: "Ed, you're a great guy and people really like you, but I just don't know if you've got what it takes to lead this group. The team is concerned which makes me concerned." While Ed's focus on using humor to connect with the team was great, he didn't take the time to establish the necessary credibility with them.

Learning the Lesson:

Any one of us can think about an influential figure we've had in our lives, whether a parent, boss, or religious leader, who used humor to build camaraderie and inspire people. Leaders who have a sense of humor motivate those around him to want to participate in the journey. The problem arises, though, when a leader tries to connect with a team of people prior to establishing himself as *worthy* of being followed. If a leader fails to establish his worthiness by gaining credibility with the team, the team may only stick with the leader when things are going well and there are no problems on the horizon. The moment that problems start cropping up, team members will be more apt to defect because they won't have faith in the leader to navigate the storm. *Credibility breeds acceptance, humor fosters inspiration.*

So why is the failure to establish credibility such a massive issue? Here are the biggies:

- **Team members need to trust that the leader can get from origin to destination** – Being a leader means knowing the plan and leading the team down the field. The leader not only needs to know the plan and how to execute, she needs to communicate the plan to the team and ensure the team understands and believes in the plan.

- **Team members need to feel secure that the leader will navigate well through stormy issues** – Think of an airline flight you've been on where some unexpected turbulence hit. While the plane is rocking and rolling, the pilot speaks to the passengers with incredible calmness and control. His job is to make you feel that things are well in hand. Imagine if turbulence hit and you heard the pilot say "We've got problems and I'm not sure what to do!" I'd be heading to the cockpit to fly the bird myself (and I can barely fly a kite never mind a plane!) Having credibility with the team gives the team greater security that the leader will get them through sticky issues.

- **Use of humor by a credibility-starved leader will exacerbate the credibility issue** – When leaders continually use humor as a means to connect with a team without establishing credibility up-front, the use of humor itself becomes a credibility inhibitor. Teams will tend to see the use of humor as the leader trying to "cover up" the fact that he may not know what he is doing. Thus, each time the credibility-starved leader cracks a joke, he is actually reinforcing this lack of credibility issue with the team. Rather than seizing the opportunity to gain credibility, the leader uses it to brush up on his lounge act.

Adding it up:

Appropriate use of humor is a great means to inspire a team to perform, so long as the credibility has already been established. Use the following tips to help you get over the credibility hump:

- **Start with listening –** Gaining credibility doesn't mean you have all the answers before you understand the questions. In fact, not taking the time to listen can actually hurt your credibility campaign and brand you as arrogant (we'll talk more about this in lesson #2). Demonstrating a clear understanding of team concerns and issues is a great credibility builder in that the team learns to trust you as a leader.

- **Use humor sparingly up front –** The team first and foremost wants to know why they should be following you. Use those initial opportunities with the team to connect through understanding the issues they are facing and gaining an understanding of the most important things for you as a leader to focus on. As you build the credibility, feel free to introduce more humor to move the team from *accepting* you to being *inspired* to follow you.

- **Don't be so gun-shy of using humor that you are viewed as a stick-in-the-mud** – Being cautious about using humor shouldn't give you a reputation as stern, mean, or stoic. By all means, be pleasant, approachable, and engaged in your interaction. The team will find it easier to talk to you and will get a more comfortable feeling that you understand their problems.

- **Use a bit of self-deprecating humor** – I use this technique a lot particularly when I am doing presentations. I will frequently tell of a situation where I did something really foolish or where I publicly embarrassed myself in front of a group of people. This demonstrates that you're secure enough with your own abilities to share them with other people. It also shows that you are able to laugh at *yourself* and not take yourself too seriously. One note of caution here: don't be self-deprecating to a point that the team sees you as having a self-esteem issue.

- **Avoid humor which tarnishes the credibility of others** – Using humor which trashes other people or competitors creates problems in a couple of ways for you as a leader. The first has to do with the trustworthiness of the leader. While team members may see destructive jokes as funny, they can develop a viewpoint of "so what does this person say about *me* when I'm not in the room?" The second has to do with the questionability of your motivations. When you trash talk others for a laugh, you can be viewed as attempting to build your credibility at the expense of someone else through your own insight and wit. For credibility to be well entrenched in the team it needs to be absolute, not relative. Otherwise, you're only demonstrating that you are worthy to lead a team until someone better or smarter comes along. Not a good foundation to establish credibility.

Graduating with honors:
Look, none of us wants to follow a leader with all the personality of cottage cheese. Having a leader who is able to share an occasional joke and laugh with a team is huge in moving a team from *acceptance* to *inspiration*. Just ensure that you as a leader take the first step to establish credibility with the team and garner their trust in you before you get too liberal with the funny stuff.

See a sample chapter from *Six-Word Lessons for Project Managers: 100 Lessons to Make You a Better Project Manager*

Know the Problem, Define the Need

1

Can't write down problem, kill project.

If the Project Sponsor cannot clearly articulate the problem, don't bother proceeding.

Get the sponsor or designee to physically write down the problem statement for all to understand.

2

Sponsor feels problem pain, project on!

Projects that are worth doing mean the sponsor feels some pain that the project can cure.

Make sure you have the right sponsor who feels the benefit of project success and the pain of status quo.

3

Team doesn't understand problem. Build what?

When the team doesn't understand the problem the likelihood of a satisfactory solution is left to chance.

Take the time to ensure the team understands the problem the way the sponsor understands the problem.

4

Sponsor doesn't care about problem. Thud.

A problem that is no longer on the sponsor's radar means it will die a slow death.

Things change. Make sure the sponsor still considers the problem a priority and one which needs to be fixed now.

5

Requirements unclear: team gets to decide.

Unclear requirements leave too much interpretation up to the team which results in building the wrong solution.

Take the time to ensure the requirements are clearly understood and agreed upon among all parties.

Bad requirements: do bad stuff faster.

Poorly written requirements can cause you to build a solution that just does stupid things faster.

Don't accept requirements which are of poor quality or don't focus on solving the stated problem.

7

Requirements are outdated. Still using microfilm?

Requirements written eons ago may not apply in the world here and now and very likely won't meet the current need.

Do take advantage of work previously done; just make sure the requirements are relevant for today and tomorrow.

8

Business evolves. Do requirements keep up?

Business changes cause even the most current requirements to change; ignoring change means weak solution.

Be cognizant of sudden or anticipated changes and ensure the requirements reflect the new business environment.

9

Problem not measurable. Solution not doable.

A problem that cannot be quantified makes solving the problem highly subjective and more subject to failure.

Ensure there are clear and objective criteria for knowing that the problem was solved. No squishy criteria.

More Books by Lonnie Pacelli

Want to be a leader others admire? Get the 12 simple leadership lessons the best leaders crush in *Why Don't They Follow Me?*

Want to be more disability inclusive but don't know where to start? You need the seven steps in *Behind Gold Doors-Seven Steps to Create a Disability Inclusive Organization*

Need to deliver projects on time, budget, and within scope? Get 100 lessons to make you a better project manager in *Six-Word Lessons for Project Managers*

Want to know how to avoid the project guillotine? Get 100 lessons to avert failure in *Six-Word Lessons to Avoid Project Disaster*

Want to know what it really means to be a great project sponsor? See how and more in the *Project Management Screw-Ups Series*

Are you guilty of the seven deadly sins of leadership? See this and more in the *Straight Talk Leadership Seminars*

Want to be the type of leader who people *want* to follow? Get 75 lessons the best leaders use to deliver results in *Lead Already!*

See Lonnie's Amazon Backlist at LPacelli.com.

See more about Lonnie at LonniePacelli.com

www.ingramcontent.com/pod-product-compliance
Lightning Source LLC
Chambersburg PA
CBHW022121280326
41933CB00007B/482